CONTENTS

WHAT IS AN OCEAN?

Nearly three-quarters of the Earth's **surface** is covered by water. Most of the water on Earth is **salt water**, found in seas and oceans. The rest is **fresh water**, found in lakes and rivers.

This picture of Earth was taken from space. From far away, we can see how much water there is on Earth. The blue is the water and the white is clouds.

Arctic Ocean

North America

Europe

Asia

Atlantic Ocean

Pacific Ocean

Africa

equator

South America

Pacific Ocean

Indian Ocean

Australasia and Oceania

Southern Ocean

Antarctica

An ocean is a large area of salt water. All of the salt water on Earth is connected, but we think of it as five different oceans.

The five oceans on Earth are called the Arctic Ocean, the Atlantic Ocean, the Indian Ocean, the Pacific Ocean and the Southern Ocean. Look at the map and find out which ocean is furthest north.

FACT CAT FACT

Each litre of water in the ocean contains 0.000000013 grams of gold. Across all the world's oceans, this adds up to around 20 **million** tonnes of gold!

WHAT IS A SEA?

A sea is a part of an ocean. Every ocean contains several seas. Seas are usually close to land.

The Caribbean Sea is part of the Atlantic Ocean. Look at the map on the next page – can you find the Caribbean Sea?

There are more than one hundred seas on Earth. Most of them are in the Pacific Ocean and the Atlantic Ocean.

This map shows some of the seas on Earth. Not all seas have the word 'sea' in their name. Look at the map and find an example.

Arctic Ocean

Greenland Sea

Barents Sea

East Siberian Sea

Norwegian Sea

Gulf of Alaska

Hudson Bay

Labrador Sea

Irish Sea

North Sea

Celtic Sea

English Channel

Bering Sea

Gulf of Mexico

Atlantic Ocean

Mediterranean Sea

Yellow Sea

Sea of Japan

Pacific Ocean

Caribbean Sea

equator

Red Sea

Arabian Sea

Bay of Bengal

South China Sea

Philippine Sea

Pacific Ocean

Gulf of Guinea

Indian Ocean

Timor Sea

Coral Sea

Scotia Sea

Tasman Sea

Southern Ocean

FACT CAT FACT

The water in the Yellow Sea is actually yellow! Its colour comes from sand and clay in the water.

COASTLINES

A coastline is the area where an ocean or a sea meets the land. Some coastlines have beaches made up of sand or **pebbles**.

Some coastlines have tall **cliffs**. These rocky cliffs are on the Atlantic coast of Portugal.

FACT CAT FACT

The total length of all the coastlines on Earth is 312,000 kilometres. Find out which country has the longest coastline.

Waves and wind move sand and pebbles along the coastline. This can **damage** the **habitat** of the animals and plants that live on the beach.

Small fences called groynes help to keep sand and pebbles in place.

groyne

WAVES

Waves are made when wind moves across the surface of the ocean. Most waves form in the middle of the ocean, and then move towards land.

These small waves are in the middle of the ocean.

Waves **break** when they reach **shallow water** near the coastline.

The size of a wave depends on the strength of the wind. Tall waves are good for watersports, such as surfing. Always ask an adult before going into rough water, because it can be dangerous.

This surfer is riding breaking waves on a surfboard.

FACT CAT FACT

Surfing originally comes from Hawaii and the Polynesian islands in the Pacific Ocean. Find out what the first surfboards were made of.

THE OCEAN FLOOR

The bottom of the ocean is called the ocean floor. Near the coast, the ocean isn't very deep. The ocean floor is only a few hundred metres from the surface.

Some ocean plants and animals live in **shipwrecks** on the ocean floor.

shipwreck

In the middle of the ocean, the ocean floor can be thousands of metres from the surface. It is so **deep** that sunlight can't reach it, so this part of the ocean is very dark and cold.

This phantom anglerfish lives close to the ocean floor, in deep parts of the Atlantic and Southern Oceans.

FACT CAT FACT

The Mariana Trench is the deepest point in the ocean. It is more than 11 kilometres deep. Find out which ocean the Mariana Trench is in.

TROPICAL SEAS

Tropical seas are found near the equator. The water there is warm, and often home to coral reefs.

The Great Barrier Reef is the largest coral reef in the world. Find out which sea it is found in.

The Arabian Sea and the Red Sea are tropical seas in the Indian Ocean. People visit the coastlines of these two seas to go swimming and snorkelling.

Sharm el-Sheikh is a city on the Egyptian coast of the Red Sea. Its beaches are very popular with **tourists**.

FACT CAT FACT

The Red Sea is one of the saltiest seas in the world.

POLAR SEAS

The seas around the **North Pole** and the **South Pole** are called **polar seas**. They are the coldest seas on Earth, and are covered in ice for most of the year.

Icebergs sometimes break away from the ice on the water's surface. They can be dangerous to ships. Find out the name of the ship that was sunk by an iceberg in 1912.

FACT CAT FACT

Only a very small part of an iceberg is above the water. Most of it is hidden underwater.

On top of the ice, the temperature is around -60 °C. It is much warmer underwater, with temperatures of between -2 and 10 °C.

White whales, or belugas, live near the coasts of polar seas in the Arctic Ocean.

TEMPERATE SEAS

Temperate seas are found between polar and tropical seas. They are warm in some places and cold in others.

Puffins build their nests on the coastlines of temperate seas, such as the Norwegian Sea. Find a country in which people eat puffins.

The UK is **surrounded** by four temperate seas: the North Sea, the Irish Sea, the Celtic Sea and the English Channel.

Every year, more than 3.6 million **passengers** travel across the Irish Sea by **ferry**.

The English Channel is only 32 kilometres wide at its **narrowest** point, so sometimes people swim across it. The fastest time anyone has swum across the Channel in is 7 hours.

HOW WE USE THE OCEAN

Most of the fish that we eat is caught in **nets** by fishermen on large fishing boats.

This fisherman is taking fish out of a net by hand. On large boats, machines are used to do this job.

FACT CAT FACT

More than 77 billion kilograms of fish and shellfish are caught from the ocean every year. This is the same weight as nearly 13 million elephants!

Fuels, such as oil and gas, **form naturally** under the ocean floor. When fuels are burned, they make energy that powers cars and heats buildings.

We can collect oil and gas using giant oil rigs. This oil rig is in the North Sea. Find out which ocean the North Sea is in.

QUIZ

Try to answer the questions below. Look back through the book to help you. Check your answers on page 24.

1 How many oceans are there on Earth?

a) 6
b) 5
c) 8

2 An ocean is part of a sea. True or not true?

a) true
b) not true

3 Which country does surfing come from?

a) South Africa
b) Australia
c) Hawaii and the Polynesian islands

4 Which ocean is the Arabian Sea in?

a) The Indian Ocean
b) The Southern Ocean
c) The Atlantic Ocean

5 Most of an iceberg is above the water. True or not true?

a) true
b) not true

6 Oil and gas are found under the ocean floor. True or not true?

a) true
b) not true

GLOSSARY

billion one thousand million (1,000,000,000)

break when a wave reaches its highest point before falling forwards into the ocean

cliff high, steep rocks that form a coast

coral a hard material made by a very small sea animal

coral reef a tropical sea habitat made from coral

damage to harm something

deep when the top and the bottom of something are far apart

equator an imaginary line around the middle of the Earth

ferry a ship that regularly carries passengers across water

form to make or create

fresh water water with no salt in it

fuel something we burn to make power or heat

habitat the area where an animal or a plant lives

iceberg a large piece of ice in the ocean

million one thousand thousand (1,000,000)

narrow something with a small distance between its two sides

naturally when something happens as part of nature, and is not created by humans

net a material made of crossed threads

North Pole the most northern point on Earth

passenger someone who is travelling in a vehicle, but not driving it

pebble a small stone

polar sea a sea located near the North or the South Pole, with temperatures of between -2 and 10 °C

salt water water that contains salt

shallow when the top and the bottom of something are close together

shipwreck a damaged ship that has sunk to the ocean floor

South Pole the most southern point on Earth

surface the top part of something

surround to be entirely around something

temperate sea a sea located between polar and tropical seas, with temperatures of between 10 and 20 °C

tourist someone who visits a place on holiday and doesn't live there

tropical sea a sea located near to the equator, with temperatures of between 20 and 28 °C

INDEX

ANSWERS

Pages 4-20

Page 4: The Arctic Ocean

Page 7: Some examples include the Gulf of Mexico and the Bay of Bengal

Page 9: Canada

Page 11: Wood

Page 13: The Pacific Ocean

Page 14: The Coral Sea

Page 16: *The Titanic*

Page 18: Iceland or the Faroe Islands

Page 21: The Atlantic Ocean

Quiz answers

1 b) 5

2 b) not true, a sea is a part of an ocean

3 c) Hawaii

4 a) The Indian Ocean

5 b) not true, most of an iceberg is hidden below the water

6 a) true